MW0637026

Horse Medicine

Doug Anderson

Horse Medicine

Doug Anderson

Barrow Street Press
New York City

Designed by Robert Drummond
Cover photo by Doug Anderson
Author photo by Trish Crapo

Published 2015 by Barrow Street, Inc., a not-for-profit
(501) (c) 3) corporation. All contributions are tax deductible.
Distributed by:
    Barrow Street Books
    P.O. Box 1558
    Kingston, RI 02881

Barrow Street Books are also distributed by Small Press Distribution,
SPD, 1341 Seventh Street Berkeley, CA 94710-1409, spd@spdbooks.org;
(510) 524-1668, (800) 869-7553 (Toll-free within the US); amazon.com;
Ingram Periodicals Inc., 1240 Heil Quaker Blvd, PO Box 7000,
La Vergne TN 37086-700 (615) 213-3574; and Armadillo & Co.,
7310 S. La Cienega Blvd, Inglewood, CA 90302, (310) 693-6061.

Special thanks to the University of Rhode Island English Department
and especially the PhD Program in English, 60 Upper College Road,
Swan 114, Kingston, RI 02881, (401) 874-5931, which provides
valuable in-kind support, including graduate and undergraduate interns.

First Edition

Library of Congress Control Number: 2015935112

ISBN 978-0-9893296-6-8

For Pam and Paul and the Herd.

CONTENTS

Part I

THE TEMPLE   3
BINGE   4
ELEMENTS   5
MY ENEMY   6
THE MASS GRAVES AT HUẾ   7
BRICOLEURS   8
SAME OLD   9
LONG BEACH, MARCH 1968   10
IT AIN'T OVER   11
LETTING GO   12
PETITIONARY PRAYER ON NGUYEN DUY'S ROOF   13
ICON   14
ROUGH BEAST   15
AND THE GREATEST OF THESE IS LOVE   16
WAITING FOR THE MARRIAGE COUNSELOR   17
THE DEAD   18
SMALL CARDIAC TREATISE   19
THE HARD, HARD THING   20
MEMPHIS, 1970   21

Part II

LETTER TO MARTÍN ESPADA   25
WHAT THE ANGEL SAID   27
LISTEN   28
AT THE FOOT OF THE VOLCANO   29
ROOD SHADOW   30
SALVATION   33
ARS POETICA   34
POETRY READING   35
MISSI SEPPE   36
RETURN   38

WINGS OF DESIRE   39

CAFÉ   40

PLAINSONG   41

SOOTHER   43

BIRDS   44

DRUNK   45

BAD MEDITATOR   46

DEAR SAPPHO   48

SCATTERING MY MOTHER'S ASHES ON THE
    FAMILY PLOT AT HICKMAN, KENTUCKY   49

KIND OF BLUE   50

LIVE MYTH   51

HORSE MEDICINE   52

ONE WOMAN ON A TALL HORSE,
    THE OTHER ON THE GROUND   53

RAINING IN THE FIELDS   54

MARE   55

SEVENTY   56

MELANCHOLY   57

LA VIDA ES CORTA, PERO AMPLIA   58

WHAT NOW   59

NORTHERN LIGHTS   60

THEORY   62

BREAKING THROUGH   63

PRACTICE THIS   64

MAGNOLIA   65

UNTITLED   66

SIXTY-ONE   67

ODYSSEUS   68

TO THE YOUNG STUDS AT THE GYM   69

NOT IMPORTANT   70

THESEUS   71

PSALM   72

ACKNOWLEDGMENTS

Part I

THE TEMPLE

For Nguyen Duy, Ho Chi Minh City, 2000

At the temple in Saigon
your daughter said to me,
When I am sad I go to the Buddhists
and when I am happy
I go to the Catholics
and I think, how Quan Yin
blurs with Mary
then comes into focus as Lan Anh,
your daughter, a child of the war
and a gift to your sweet spirit.
When we were walking
out of the temple yard
she said, Look,
there is an old man
by a cage of finches.
If you give him a dollar
he will free one bird.
And then she says,
Look up in the trees
where the finches
gather on a low branch
when they are freed, and wait
to come back to the cage
where they feel safe.
And I think, yes,
this country, that war,
how it has become a home for me.
I carry it on my back wherever I go
and gather it around me when I sleep.

BINGE

War comes to visit me once a day.
I can't get rid of him.
He's grown old and hates himself.
I stopped a quarter century ago,
but he still drinks—sits in airport bars
and watches the cocky uniforms
line up at the departure gates.
Desert camouflage this time, tan boots.
He orders another double and snickers,
little eyes set close together
in too large a head, like a grizzly's,
opaque and dead. Flies swarm
around his gore-smeared muzzle.
He stinks of corpse. I let him sleep in the garage.
You see, there's no way to make him leave.
Go to war just once, he's always with you.
At breakfast he feels like he's got
an ice pick in his head, swears off the stuff.
Never again, he says, I've found God.
By five he's back in the blood glow of the bar,
bumming drinks and telling lies.
He's got an eye for boys and girls
with wallets full of combat pay.
He'll Mickey Finn them,
roll them for their souls and go off giggling.
I see Senator Goldmouth weaving
down the bar to slap him on the back:
Let freedom ring! says he,
teeth twinkling from the neon at the bar.

ELEMENTS

The typhoon spins tin roofs off shacks
and sends them scything.
Where sea meets river mouth,
the swollen mingling
washes away whole villages,
people sucked under in their sleep.
It has been raining for a week.
Leeches spill from flood surge
into the paddies and we burn them off
with cigarettes. Watch them drop and writhe.
The mines we just put down and armed
are shifting in the turbid water
and we fear to step on them ourselves.
Our weapons jam with grit and rust.
The heat falls away, we shiver in our ponchos,
try to light sodden cigarettes.
There, a dog stands on a hummock,
cut off from home, where they will eat him.
He shakes and sprays and lives another day.
We wade through rice fertilized with human shit.
The leeches come back and we burn them off again.
There, Smithson stands butt naked, killing them,
his thighs streaming with blood.
That night we light Sterno tabs and heat coffee.
The rain roars in the leaves.
I would not wish this on my enemy,
out there trying to make a fire to cook his rice.

MY ENEMY

Quang Nam Province, 1967

We imagined him as wily, reptilian,
squatting in a hole alive with snakes,
or underwater breathing through a reed,
his gelding knife glimmering in the green,
leering with the cruelty he'd inflict on us
if he overran our lines. But now,
see this prisoner two-thirds our height,
gray-faced, legs caked with mud,
ribs showing, his rotten teeth
outsize in his shrunk skull. How he
stands there in the rain, dazed, perhaps
looking past the torture to his death
and maybe there, he'll find some sense to this.

THE MASS GRAVES AT HUẾ

After the siege of Huẻ and the enemy withdrawal,
it was impossible to tell which dead were ARVN,
NVA, or civilian, blackened as they were.
And so those who buried them, kind in their exhaustion,
wearing cloth masks against the stench and
pushed beyond all thought into the realm of ghosts,
dragged the bodies into mass graves and covered them,
without regard to who they were and where they stood
in this long and mindless war, and so as the land
became fertile there, the vines and flowers thrived.
Would that our dead have been buried
with them and our brotherhood be known.

BRICOLEURS

We who admired Pound's poetry
are talking about being

embarrassed by his politics and then
I remember the Vietnamese who told me

The French taught us how to grow cotton,

and pointed at the American truck engine
that ran a pump

and brought clear water to the rice.
He smiled and showed

his yellow, intermittent teeth
from living in the jungle all those years,

eating what he could find,
smoking butts left by GIs

and drinking from the craters made by bombs.

SAME OLD

On radio watch I'd see tracers floating
above the horizon, arc light
in the mountains and then seconds later,
the rumble. All far away.
I'd be grateful to not be way over there,
mosquitoes my near and only enemy.
But next noon when we were in it
and there was no night for cover,
facedown in a dry paddy with mortars
walking in and a crossfire of two snipers
pinning us flat in the heat, our artillery
taking its time, and somebody
shouting CORPSMAN UP, me getting up
to run and maybe die: there's no poetry
in that, only the immediate choking fear.
Came home to a country that watched
the war on TV at dinner. No one put down
their forks: it was all in a box,
an electronic terrarium for detached
observation. These same folks
(or their children) just keep on voting in
the clowns who'd happily make us die
over and over again, the teenage fools
who buy the snake oil one more time.
I could get a resentment over this
but no one would listen, leastwise
the ones fattening on the war.
Always a war somewhere and underneath
the crack of rifles, the sound of money
sliding down the chute, and a
whimpering of mothers over here, over there.

LONG BEACH, MARCH 1968

A whole barracks full of combat vets
waiting to be discharged—we'd been
mustered in to hear a young lieutenant
lecture us on all the goodies we would get
if we re-upped. Had this single ribbon
on his chest, shoes polished to a mirror,
nice creases in his pants and I felt bad
for him standing up there in a room
full of people he'd be afraid to meet
in town at night, trailing something dark
behind us as we walked under the streetlights.
Felt worse for him still when he looked up
and smiled at us and someone
way in back bounced a spitball off his chest.

IT AIN'T OVER

Some things are over before they're over.
A bad marriage. A bad war.
It got so a squad would go out,
call in checkpoints as if on the move,
sit down in a ravine and wait it out.
Down south they'd started killing officers
while they slept, a grenade rolled under them
by men who'd had enough of being sent
out into hell for other people's money.
The friend that writes you he loves you
but can no longer abide the war.
A fistful of joints soaked in opium
costs a dollar, starts looking pretty good.
When I left, I thought I'd died
and the afterlife was made up
of clean sheets and food that didn't come
from a can left over from another war.
Couldn't sleep. Even when a woman held my heart.

LETTING GO

For Bảo Ninh

I asked him how he could not hate us.
We killed his children and left his country
a sump of chemicals and upturned graves.
Ten years in the jungle, hammered by
two-thousand-pound bombs. His job,
to gather his comrades' body parts
into something like a whole, to bury them.
He said, *We had the Chinese*
for a thousand years, and then the French,
the Japanese. You are merely the most recent.
He lit a cigarette and looked out into the smoky bar.
Finally, and I believed him, he said,
We have nothing left to hate you with.

PETITIONARY PRAYER ON
NGUYEN DUY'S ROOF

Saigon, January 2000

Black sky and moon of chipped ice.
We fall on the chicken, the shrimp,
the sliced melons. The whiskey
picks up the neon from the streets.
A sudden breeze cools our damp shirts.
Below, children play in the light
from open doorways.
The heat of the day has made us silent.
Lan Anh, in her simple white dress, pours tea.
God, make me young again and not stupid.

ICON

So full of rage to look on
the statue's smug serenity
I struck the Buddha with
a pry bar, hard, and out of
the horrible fissure
rushed the dark water
that had been mulling there,
the bloodied blossoms
of a tree whose roots
crushed my heart, the faces
of all we killed in that war
and were killed by,
then a hand formed from a cloud
presented me with a necklace
of skulls, heavy, heavy,
and I was paid one dollar
for each death and the money
tore my pockets,
pulled me under the water
that now roared into a river
and everyone I hated
came floating by
and I could not help but love them.

ROUGH BEAST

On a troublesome poem of Yeats

We are aware that Jackboot Jack,
if not kept busy rutting at the bar,
will outshout the quieter music,
trample the part of us that knows
we can't kill off our ugly spirit
but strive to soothe his arrogance,
fill his cage with mirrors
so he doesn't see the bars,
merely licks and rubs himself
upon them. We do not lack
all conviction, but neither do we
let him take his bludgeon out
into the night to cloud the rain
with blood. His passionate intensity
is neither passion nor intensity
but a knife sunk in the heart's eye.
How simple to kill off the mind-snakes
we've invested others with,
without knowing we are the venom.
It *should* make him slouch,
but far away from Bethlehem
into the desert to be burned away to ash
and scattered by the wind.
He's best kept close where we can see him,
humor him in his reptilian play.
It's called being human,
and it's a ploy, but it keeps us whole,
this double soul, this responsibility.

AND THE GREATEST OF THESE IS LOVE

I saw the Pentecostals when the spirit struck them
get out of their van and rush
to the downed power line as it popped and sparked,
snake-whipping back and forth
on the road between two lines of cop-stopped cars.
Yes, unheeding the spirit-struck got out and danced
with the blue tongue of it
in spite of the shouts and gasps
and how they jigged harder when it bit them
and what was almost funny but not quite
was how they jerked around
all angles and elbows and cut puppet strings
their faces white-hot and God-boggled.
How clumsy we are in love
how we cannot dance with it except for a short while before
it forks toward farce or flight and how magnificent
when we are able to let it drift close to the water
like a seagull touching down and lifting up.

WAITING FOR THE MARRIAGE COUNSELOR

The skeletal bride and groom in the little glass box.
The sugar skulls.
Let us love one another and not wake the graveyard
        with our bickering.
How we make war on our lives: as if we deserve
        more than a gleam of light caught in the fall
        from womb to grave.
Scrabbling all the way for our portion of the longing.
That night in the desert reaching up to pick
        the cold fruit of the sky.
The flesh tangle of our loving that would look
        on film so slapstick and yet for us
        was that one pair of angels who in the great expulsion
        flew up above heaven instead.
Help me up the hill and, yes, you will need me too.
And, blessedly, let us shut up and love the imperfection
        of our ripening past sell-by.
There, that bird. And our old blind dog. And the tomato
        from your garden cut perfectly in half.
Our hands folded like birds waiting for the storm.

THE DEAD

The train leaves nightly. I wave to the faces pressed against the glass.
There Sandy, there Joe, there Jack. Suzanne of the cobalt blue eyes
and beautiful breasts, I know them all. Bill and Newton and Birdie.
Each night when they arrive I knock on the windows and ask,
What is it like over there? They answer, mouths moving,
but I can't hear them and so they hold up crude drawings
scrawled on lined paper: an apple, a fish, a cup of coffee,
a child's bright sun. The drawings come alive:
the wind flattening then caressing the grass.
Seagulls hunkered down and waiting for a storm and, Oh,
the sweet sideways light of afternoon touching and reddening yet more
the old brick buildings along 11th Avenue. A pear ripening
and a jar of honey making a wavering pool of gold on the wooden table.
I press my ear to the glass. The boarding line I'm standing in
gets shorter as the world behind me fills with laughter.
The train pulls away. I button my top button against the cold.

SMALL CARDIAC TREATISE

Broken heart, heartless, fainthearted, heart on sleeve.
Can't use those, even though the conditions they describe
are as water to its word. The Latin, *Cor*, so much like Core,
the point in us from which we all unravel,
this bouquet of neurons in the chest—might as well
write about the moon and why does this subject
magnetize my waters? Heart-tide coming in, going out:
one day good, next I might as well be having tea with Mr. Mort.
In a black winter night the heart reddens the clouds
in its psalm-rise and insomnia is prayer.
Dame valor, mi corazón, Coraje, si, and lionhearted
by fool light I will step off the cliff and fly.

THE HARD, HARD THING

You don't get over it in spite
of wonderpill, don't get
to lay your burden down.
But you can find a place for it
beside a river, in a flowering field.
You can let it off its leash
where it's not as like to bite
another's hurt, but wander,
drink deep, or sleep in the sun,
head resting on your shoulder.

MEMPHIS, 1970

Came home from that war trailing death like ground fog.
Wandered summers, did trim carpentry in Texas, bartending,
landed in Memphis working for a marble mill
where with old Thomas (eighty, born of a slave child)
I cleaned fancy mausoleums of rich folk in the graveyard.
Where old Goldmouth had leaked down from his coffin
and stained the marble I'd sand and clean
and make brand new and after, go home
to the rooming house and pull my quart of gin
from the toilet tank where I hid it from the crone
who took the rent and snooped.
Some memories are like those songs that get stuck
in your head and won't leave.
I thought I'd write it out and kill it off.
But what did it was turning seventy-one last year
and thinking about how the lights
are going out behind me and catching up.
Who'd want a tomb? Someplace where those
who probably hated old Goldmouth still come,
pretend to do homage and instead look both ways and spit.
I thought about how we cling to the self:
a grave where others come to remember you,
a place to have a name and presence still.
And I thought how clean are ashes and how fine
to have them flung somewhere out in the field where maybe
you fell in love, and gave your best, for all the wildflowers, yes.

Part II

LETTER TO MARTÍN ESPADA

No ese realismo mágico

Dear Martín:

In Izalco, while Christ waits for Easter
in his glass tomb in the cathedral
a single long note is blown on a trumpet
en el parque central. Los perros flacos
forage at the feet of la gente.
Los poetas mount the stage in a shower of rose petals
thrown by old ladies.
The mayor opens his arms wide.
in the audience are campesinos, hijitos, shopkeepers,
viejos, the town trauma surgeon, and a generous contingent
of la policia con pistolas, escopetas y M16s.
Solamente el volcán duerme esta noche.
Los perros flacos jump into the big blue garbage cans.
Martín, you will certainly believe this.
Each poeta is introduced with a fireworks rocket.
Los perros flacos jump out of the big blue garbage cans.
Poetas de Argentina, Taiwan, Guatemala, España,
Peru, Nicaragua, France, Costa Rica, Brazil, Venezuela, Chile y
Los Estados Unidos open their mouths.
Out come pajaros, serpientes y duendes,
hombres, mujeres y alquimistas with flasks of ether.
Out come revolutionaries in diapers, ambassadors
in limousines of obsidian, the Virgin in a Madonna T-shirt
y los indios with flutes made of thighbones
and bombs made of skulls; out come
the dead dictators chained together by ectoplasm
swinging censers that emit the stink of money,
priests with rifles, nuns with giant beasts
whose names are forgotten hidden in the musk
of their habits; out come conquistadores on roller skates,
Moros in black on black motorcycles, Mad Max

with tattoos de los Mara Salvatrucha.
When los poetas have finished, there are more fireworks.
They are swarmed by hijitos, viejos y otros
wanting autographs. Their hands are soft as their hearts.
Death does not hide here but lives among them dressed in
white lace with earrings rattling on her skull. Life does not hide
here but steps through irony as if it were a vanishing fog.

WHAT THE ANGEL SAID

You may
have to die this time

to speak truth,
may have to

be driven
into the wilderness

of your own land
where things have gone

far beyond remedy.
When it falls,

and when the earth
has sucked the bones

long enough
your song will be heard.

Sometimes it's that way:
Who are you to think

you will not have to
live history

out all the way
to the consequences

and beyond?
That holocausts

would pass you by
when no others were spared?

And by the way,
Who are you if not

someone to carry your share?
Oh heavy, heavy.

LISTEN

Not the sideways rain that whips against the windows
but a steady, garden-soaking murmur: would I were that
and not the shivering heath-walker with fork-lit heart.
There the horses crop the meadow as before,
but soaked, enjoying this respite from the flies.
Listen: a rivulet in the tangle of the slope, and a bird,
even in this, pings and primps. It's been a while
since I've lain awake with her, skin to skin and wordless.

AT THE FOOT OF THE VOLCANO

They believe you when you tell them that just over the hill
        there is a cyclops
feeding on the carcass of a saint.
They go over the hill and see that you are lying.
You tell them that the revolution will come and that all
        the land will be distributed equally.
They do not believe you now.
In their church the Virgin occupies the largest space
behind the altar   Christ, down front, is smaller.
You point this out and receive no response   their eyes
        become dull in your presence.
At Easter, Christ is carried around the village in a large
        glass tomb.
Walk behind and flog yourself with barbed wire   by Lent
        they believe you again.
Unless you lie once more in which case   barbed wire
        will not be sufficient.
In my country we lie all the time   it makes a pleasant noise.

ROOD SHADOW

They get Jesus
in a back room

at the country club,
tell him,

let's get you in some
Armani

and could you
step over there

and wash your feet?
Maybe we can

get you a pedicure.
See

we want you
to be able to walk into

our churches
without

upsetting all those folks
in their Sunday best,

we want you to fit in,
grace the board meeting

once in a while
and we want you to look good on TV

(Got to do something about
that coif)

so when you tell
all those liberal pervs

to straighten up
or hell's awaitin'

we want you to have AUTHORITY
and we want to

market a version of you
to our less educated folks

that shoots lightning
out your fingertips

at homos and these bitches
who want

ownership of their own
pussies,

because we need the votes,
see,

we want heaven on Earth
and botox too,

we want the eternal Barbies
of the ass-fuck-cum-in-the-face,

we want the holy star
of the Mercedes

hood ornament
to rise on Christmas

over the Hall of Mammon,
and don't get any ideas

about fishes and loaves
or kicking the moneylenders

out of the temple, cause,
well, you know,

we've got the nails,
we've got the tree.

SALVATION

I don't believe you, there, with your miter and jeweled shoes
but I believe the woman with the dirty feet kneeling there before
little homemade shrine, face wet, anointed with blood and ash.

ARS POETICA

Like the doe you surprise that freezes when you freeze, its tail twitching.

I know that even if I move my eyes the deer will bolt. I hold her eyes with mine.

But I exhale and the pattern on my shirt moves, and there she goes zigging and leaping, then she's gone in the green dark.

We are newly naked together and you have your thigh across me, your breath on my neck, and yes, the way you tuck your toes under my calf. The way you touch me.

I try not to say it. The word that will send the doe running. I try, but it comes out. That word, that terrible hot ingot of a word crouched between two pronouns.

And I think, this is the only way it should be said, when you can't help it. Your whole body in the word, your heart all around it like a hand.

I free the word and see, there, where it goes bounding.

POETRY READING

He looks like a bored child in church, longing to range
outside in the meadow, in the stream, anywhere but here
at this poetry reading to which his wife has flogged him.
Mind still raw from the board meeting, the backstabbing,
the intrigue, the affair gone wrong sitting across the table
by the coffee urn and now here he is among people
who think this stuff is manna from heaven. If I could only,
he thinks, sleep with my eyes open, smile in all the right places,
if only someone would pull the fire alarm, and so he slumps
in his chair and inhales the several perfumes of the tribe.
But one line, somewhere in the middle of the first poem
has him sitting up, his spine infused with light. She said,
Finally we are together in the departure lounge,
sorting through our things, wondering what to take into
the dark, and our nakedness comes back to us whole,
and all we have loved spills out of the baggage at our feet.

MISSI SEPPE

Up north, picked up some elk antlers.
At Hickman, I drowned a drunk police chief.
Sewell's Crossing, I snapped an anchor chain
and sent the tanker *Muskrat Euphoria*
turning slowly in the current down to the Gulf.
At Tunica I sucked up pure black topsoil,
dropped it at Green Hill where they grow nothing
but golf courses. There's no malice in this.
I just dig my channel deeper every year
and you load me with more haulage, more things
that don't work. Hell, I've got a Civil War submarine
snagged in the vines down Wardens Way.
I'm not that different from you, really.
You folks supply the content and then
run around like a pinball banking off Crying Clown
and Neon Nelly when the money comes in.
Sometimes I make an oxbow and sit out for a while,
delegate my gut to grind rocks on down the delta.
I've got enough trouble with gravity
and you dam and shunt me off somewhere.
Hurricanes give me shingles.
I swell up, take out a bridge or two.
Deep down beyond where dredges reach
I roll the skulls from flu coffins that sank with a barge in 1918.
Below that, igneous rock just this side
of batholiths of white hot smelt you'll get to know some day.
Man, I can't see the sky for the dirty bottom boats
that grunt down to New Orleans slow and smug.
The fish I carry are mean as snakes; gars, catfish,
fin your hand off at the wrist.
There's an old woman, Sally Beasely, lives by her black self
on an island I carved off the bank in the last flood.
Let the house stand. Ask her anything you want to know.
She's got all the fish she wants but she has to row

a long way if she wants to go to town.
Has to row back after and hope the island's still there.
Ask *her* about uncertainty.
At Fiddler's Bridge I caught a suicide˙
and sent him back up on the bank to try again, the fool.
Tell you something while you enjoy the quiet.
You people have a ruptured sense of time.
Let this drift up to you from the hiss of water off the bow.
Turn me over and I'm Acheron.

RETURN

Hafiz, let me understand you:
even when broken by love,

when you think you'll die
and are afraid you won't,

or even when struck silly
in the first weeks before you wake

to see her with the glow worn off
and know that, like you, she is a stranger,

even then—or in grieving the loss of her
and the long longing after—in a heaven

we have not yet eyes to know,
our hearts are ripening

and it will all come back to us,
children that we are, and will be.

WINGS OF DESIRE

after Wim Wenders

The way the angels walk
down the subway car,
listen to people
who could be us, our dark songs,
ground glass obsessions,
and see that we somehow
have the gravitas to not cry out
like the street corner mad.
The way we shoulder
what we've been handed
that grows heavier
as our knees turn to dust
and how we sometimes look ahead
to death—not out of fear
but for a coming mercy—
how could they not fall in love with us
and defect, like Jesus
to the earth and be broken like him?

CAFÉ

It's early and the waitstaff are smiling.
Even the cooks are moving to the music in the back.
Out here, we are shoulder to shoulder at our little tables,
plugged in, or leaning forward into conversation,
inscribing our little zones of isolation.
Is this how it starts, the commune, the resistance?
On the way here I helped another old man
pull a dead limb from the road in front of his house.
I'm thinking we are like horses together under a big tree,
chewing, flicking our tails, mindful of a little space,
but not too much, sensing bodily warmth close enough
that in the hard times to come we may reach and touch.

PLAINSONG

Bitter cold and wind.
I turned seventy last year.
Love cupped in my hands like a lit match.

One day so tired,
so depleted of cleverness,
I was empty
and the words came
through me as if
I'd removed a boulder
from a stream.

I can't get warm this winter.
The cold comes from inside me.
What have I betrayed in myself?

We believe the sun will come up.
Spring will arrive.
This winter I am not so sure.

There is an old Chinese poet following me.
When I stop, he stops,
recedes into the shadows.
When I move again,
he moves.
The distance between us is closing

I have seen the sky so thick with stars I have wept.
Cloudless. Moonless,
But the stars, a radiant snail's trail across the black.
What can I take with me when I die?
My cupped hands.
Empty of everything but longing.

When, out of loneliness, I have taken a lover,
I have soon hurt her.
When, out of loneliness, a lover has taken me,
she has quickly wounded me.
Thank you both for being my fleshly friend
on the way to the perfection that never happens.
In a better life I would have treated you well,
and you would have held me, a charm against death.

Can I stop drowning for sirens?
Will you stop singing?

SOOTHER

It was always that lackluster and almost silent aunt,
who, instead of scowling like the rest, smiled,
or laid a hand on your shoulder, or sat and listened
to your inconsolable broken self hour after hour
and after you were restored, faded into the background
where, without complaint, she was most at home
filling in the gaps our china-breaking egos left
in the tumult of our families, forgotten, but knowing
her presence was the dark field of our constellation.

BIRDS

They don't domesticate, their little bird brains
a knot of see and eat.
No matter how long we cage them
they remain aloof. Some,
having found you harmless
will sit on a finger or a shoulder.
I had a lovebird once
that was anything but loving.
Escaped while I cleaned its cage
and went to live in the TV,
would not come out and bit me
when I tried to pry it loose.
No, they do not love us, nor did they love
St. Francis, only the seed
sprinkled on his open palm.
They are to us like people who
move to another country
and refuse to learn the language.
Or cats, who love the sofa with
its cube of sunlight more than you.
When my mother died
I sat with my friend Berta
in her living room, eating ice cream
by the pint when suddenly her cat,
feeling spry, leaped from chair to chair
and landed on the birdcage
which act so terrified the parakeet
it brained itself on the bars
and died right there.
We laughed—imagine that—
and again, loud and long,
some contraction of the gut
like grief, like the expulsion
of the bird of death from its sordid roost.

DRUNK

Another bird has flown into the glass.
They've been pecking at the fermented apples.
Farmer sent the pickers home and let the fruit
wither on the tree. It could happen to anyone.
Wake up one morning. Stare out the window.
Heart grown wild with grief.

BAD MEDITATOR

For Ellen Bass

My dog wants to go out and I want to sit with my coffee.
My back, which I threw out this weekend, is less sore.
I do not fear turning sixty-eight, which will happen
in twenty-six days, and which anyway I can do nothing about.
I like to say the word *Abba* over and over again
because the first A makes my heart buzz and then the *B*
sends me out somewhere like a handball off the wall
and then I'm brought back with the second *A*.
I once heard a mountain moan and that's no joke
and on that same day I closed my eyes
and when someone spoke the letters of their words
lit up like neon. And there, under a tree, a mons pubis
of grass was breathing. How revolutionary
we thought ourselves but we were merely seeing
what was there all the time without the pharmacopeia.
How strong our bodies and how we could do such things
and yet not die, yea verily, get up and dance.
Now I hold such things like small stones.
They are neither dimmer nor brighter than any other thing.
In fact I've grown fond of the things between the things
I used to think important. The cat called Pig
that bit people and kept coming back in spite of me
taking him ten miles out of town and leaving him.
How one time he did not come back and I was sad.
I knew an artist who discovered that the doodles he did
talking on the phone were better than the canvases
he struggled with. See, my mind has wandered.
I say *Abba*, and for a moment there is stillness
without words then it starts up all over again.
My new granddaughter, who as yet has no intellect
to impede her genius, no guile, no poisoned hopes,
has learned to wave at me and grin. I would have
dismissed this once as sentimental, skulking to the bar

to join the orgone fog in the red-light-love-murk.
My mind comes back to center where it's empty
for a blink and then I'm back to the boogie fugue
and where the strands touch, sparks.
I've read there are inner senses that are born
when the outer ones go quiet but I'm thinking how long
do I have to wait, Abba, before something is finer than
this cool slice of orange? Too long, or maybe not at all.
I'm back to center where I'm fine
for three breaths and then the dog starts to whimper.
She wants love. And I want it in spite of having it.
Late afternoon and the light is sideways and I wonder why
I am not out in it. Dear Buddha, Allah, Mahavira,
I can't abide it's all illusion, Maya, something that dissolves.
Dear Jesus and the Dalai Lama,
I love this world and will miss it where I go.

DEAR SAPPHO

Just had to have that particular orange, plump and peel-easy,
      placed at the corner of the careful pyramid,
so sent a small thunder of them across the clean green floor
      and me, not especially guilty, happy with the chosen one.

SCATTERING MY MOTHER'S ASHES
ON THE FAMILY PLOT AT HICKMAN, KENTUCKY

Down into the black, flesh curdled dirt.
Down into the family charnel,
marinade in whiskey, with the murderers
and soul murderers
against whom you honed your tongue.
Down there with the starved
and yellow-fever-sickened,
with the beans-one-day-lard-the-next-
one-foot-in-front-of-the-other life.
Down in the rivers of sodden mash
of sex-smeared hate.
With the stained wallpaper
peeled off the pale failing heart.
You burned for a while
against the cold dark and faded.
Let what continues on in the charred silence be
gentle as a baby's breath against your neck.
I wouldn't wish your life on anyone
and especially myself.
I sift the weight of you from my heart.
Take the hard words and the bloody welts
of fierce love with you.
Now that you are dead I can get a word in edgewise
but I hate long eulogies
and therefore let me
make you one like a star that has collapsed
in on itself and is so dense it can hold
everything that is said
and everything that is unsaid.
I let the last of you drift with this small wind that has made itself known
by moving the leaves as if to end this. Now.

KIND OF BLUE

Gold smelt rushing downstream setting fire to the low-hanging trees.
A whorl of hell-heaven heat carves mind glyphs in rock all the way down.
Black hands fanning the keys in the bright ground of the horn.
A hot braid of brass Trane-Nat-Cannonball, and Chambers' heartbeat.
Scatter of bones from Evans, and Jimmy Cobb, steady on, dropping coins
in the love hat of the beggar *gimme more of that so I can live.*
And so it goes with Bach-Schubert-Mahler all of them, verily,
saying there is a way out of the lopsided lobe-limp of the world
in its pit-bound course   all you have to do is fly your kite in the storm.

LIVE MYTH

I would believe in the unicorn if it stood heaving and slathered,
snapping flies off its flank with its tail. It does not smell
of sweat and stable, does not snort at the wolf in the brush
and twitch its ears. A unicorn does not get dirty,
kick up mud when it runs. I know that I would throw
my leg over a bareback horse sooner than I'd step
into the stirrup of a saddled unicorn. For spite, I'd shoot
and slaughter one, roast choice bits over a fire, and hang
its horn from my belt, just to outrage the legions
of tourists of the imagination, the kind who flock
to séances, or invite Rasputin to tea. A unicorn
is impossibly cute, it doesn't shit or rub its rump against a tree.
But a horse, my god, can swing its neck around at a dog's yip
and break your jaw, can brain you with a hoof.
It makes the ground shake. Look at him, the black pool
of his eye, muscle rippling along the flanks, and how
he stands, placid, chewing, as the little girl lies on top of him
braiding his mane, whispering, my magic, my magic, my boy.

HORSE MEDICINE

New Mexico State Prison, 1980
For Bob Doyle

Had them packed ass-over-elbow in a space
meant for half as many and the food, well,
somewhere between cardboard and baby shit,
TB and brother hepatitis living in the walls.
So understaffed the guards built snitch-world
to enforce the unenforceable. No one inside
surprised when it came down,
leastwise the guards, beaten, broken, raped.
Most inmates just wanted to survive
but the sicker meaner mutherfuckers
torched through the bars of segregation cells
and blue-flamed the pedophiles. Into which blood
waded the National Guard whence black convicts
and some others sought refuge among them in the yards
while the psychopaths dismembered snitches
with chainsaws so thoroughly that afterward
when they did the body count they couldn't find them all.
Cleaned up the blood with acid (stains still there).
Brought in a warden smart enough to build a concrete pen,
filled it with mustangs every bit as crazy
as the torch-tongued mad. Those most eaten
by their demons got to work with them, feed them,
I dare say *love* them, and for a while
something like a human village found its heartbeat
and prevailed. Warden after that took away the horses
and hell returned to what some righteous gasbag said
hell oughta be. Well there you are. And so are we.

ONE WOMAN ON A TALL HORSE, THE OTHER ON THE GROUND

That horse's ears straight up reading what I might think was silence
just beneath this heartbreaker soft breeze and the high clouds flying.
And now he's reading his mistress's conversation with the woman
on the ground, longing for that giddyap home
that forms an image in the great globe eye of the sweet green grass
in the center pen just waiting to be grazed long into the day
but now those ears pop back up to catch the Alsatian pup
bounding out of the water in a spray of diamonds
with a stick as long as herself, and then the breeze again
moving the backlit yellow leaves over the Swift River
where it comes together with the Ware
and the weaving of the waters is like a strong brown arm
torquing in the earth and opening its hand palm up to the sun.
And now the women are talking about someone who died too young,
his heart ground down and stopped by the drug
and the horse's ears are up, but open now and the grief
like warm water and the horse's heartbeat slow,
slower than ours, whispering *Listen, if you could hear what I hear,
the sorrow and the cleansing and the water whirling deep down.*

RAINING IN THE FIELDS

When a horse dies something ancient dies
that links to our beginnings after which
we'll be less than we were, less noble,
less connected to the old world
that may itself be going,
so grievously have we broken it.
The vet will come, the horse
will lie down one last time
and then the man with the backhoe
will dig a hole big enough.
You might expect to find bones beneath
the bones that will be—
something there waiting to receive
this old Pegasus. The silence here is huge,
and the grave a tunnel to another truth.

MARE

Listen to me: this Percheron
follows me up the slope
where the others gather at the hay
and we stop to talk,
or whatever it is we do.
She takes this time to drop
her huge head and pluck
imagined bugs from my coat.
I rub the long muscle just below
her mane and she folds me into her
with her neck. I think how hard it is
to manage love's rush. How sometimes
we are slapstick with it,
all hooves and teeth as big as piano keys,
tongues like sides of beef
and yet sometimes we get it right
and power puts on the glove of gentleness.
I would you knew this up front
before I touch you, kiss you,
and all that follows, that I mean my best.
Take my stampeding heart, and all the rest.

SEVENTY

Death plucks my ear / says, Live / I am coming —*Virgil*

See that fox pelt, tire pummeled dry and one red tuft wind wakened
and the way those llamas on the farm all quick-look east west north
south and then bisect the angles, nose up at some coyote's faraway funk.
Voles skittering through the crackling dead grass, the old red logging
truck, buckshot pattern on the driver's door and me now looking through
the circle made by the crane's calipers back into life at some rustling
thing—that zigging rabbit and somewhere the deep-throated bark
of a shepherd surrounded by the manic yappers, some kind of glee
I'm being offered, some kind of wake up and get my feet dirty,
pulling me in, pulling me up this village road after my long sleep,
not Van Winkle's—I've been here all along—but what a *here*
this is now, at seventy, the acolytes in black who've been putting out
the candles behind me have gone on ahead: hurry, they say, you can now
count the days to death by the number of things left after you've swept
out the crap, how much room there is now. The less of me the more
of everything worth loving: that star, that stone being rolled clack-thump
by snowmelt down the widening stream, that poem, the way that woman
lifts the hair off her neck in the heat—I want to blow on it, like a coal.

MELANCHOLY

A pear so long on the tree the sun forces out its nectar
so that wasps come and drink. Finding a mirror
left by a lover long ago and seeing myself in it.
Sun a frozen white disk in fog, and a dead limb fallen on the fence.
A dog barking in her sleep. A horse, for no reason I know,
nickering in the meadow all by himself. This me, this I,
a mere canal through which flows all the water there is
until my mask comes loose and floats away with it.
I share this water with you but somehow think my suffering
is not the same as yours. The water says it is and so
let me take the oars. Let me pull my weight in this world
of children crushed between kings in the last days of empire.

LA VIDA ES CORTA, PERO AMPLIA

(Life is short, but wide.)

I don't remember changing the oil, doing the dishes.
Do remember when I woke up with you in the bed that was too small.
Everything was new then. You. My body still forming, filling in.
Don't remember washing the car except maybe when you
leaned up against the windows on the other side to help
and I saw your breasts through your T-shirt in the window
and you saw me seeing and smiled, took off your shirt,
pressed them bare against the soapy glass.
I don't remember standing in line for my physical but
remember the first round fired at me, the whisper of it.
You can't shoehorn these things into time.
They create their own world around them.
You can't measure it. When you think of it, you step out of time
and when you return, wakened by a voice, you've been away years.
I don't remember changing the tire, cleaning the rifle, but remember
I found I could see music, could see words form
in fire when you spoke. You half naked in the front seat,
riding down to the ghost town at Malory.
Corta, yes. When I do the numbers, I know just where I am
in the continuum that will end me. I subtract. I add.
When the poet Dick Barnes was dying he didn't get serious
and start taking stock of his life but continued to do the things
that brought him pleasure: playing washboard
in the little band. Translating from the Spanish.
Loving his great-hearted wife even as he entered the final time
and began the business of pissing through his pores
because his kidneys failed. Do I have time to love again?
To have *amplia* again, to watch the landscape flare around me,
and the stars turn brighter against the cold? Stop time
and let an island form around the moment and when it is over,
back to the one foot in front of the other part, the getting by?

WHAT NOW

Jack Gilbert said our poetry changed
because we live long and long.
The romantics died too young
to face the second half of life
and all the shocks to flesh and mind
that come with that.
We watch history repeat
and our prophetic observations
bring smirks. Hardest of all,
what to do with love
when we are no longer beautiful,
when life does not want us to fan
our feathers in the sun.
And then see how the soul turns in,
makes its dark honey alone,
a lost hive hidden in a grove.

NORTHERN LIGHTS

I'd just moved up from New York
where in eight years
I'd scarcely seen the sky,
maybe one dirty star
framed between two buildings,
but nothing like this,
with the zenith cleared
by cold to perfect black.
Ice on the lake
was moaning in its labor
as it cracked and shifted
and I thought
maybe it was praising
what the three of us
looked up to see.
One whispered
"It's caused by solar storms,"
as if science would somehow
damp the awe and save us
from enchantment.
I might as well have been
the Inuit out in his kayak looking up,
the sea silent and only felt
beneath him, rocking mother.
If I'd known the words,
I'd have sung some ancient thing
and named it. Okay, I'll try:
hard to escape the signs
we've come to know it by,
say, "curtains." No,
and I say, No, such things
agreed upon too long
kill it. There is a place
in us where feeling

becomes language,
where words are hauled
out of their ovens
and the ash cleaned off,
where flesh becomes sound,
that point, where Blake said,
"My heart knock'd against
the root of my tongue"—
that place. What I saw:
magenta, yes, violet,
and stars above which
green washed over
like clear surf
above luminescence.
A robe dropping to the floor
to reveal more than
I ever wanted. Aurora
yes, who invites prayer.
Like that place
when you are first in love
and don't know
what's happening to you.
There, and where God
does not hate the body
but welcomes it back
into all it means
to be a cogitating animal
in this short life. That.
I give up. I can't speak
but only be, and be silent.

THEORY

Who does not know the word
is too slippery to own
the thing it names?
Any poet could have
told you that.
Try to nail it to the page,
it wiggles out
from underneath your pen. And irony:
if everything's ironic,
nothing is,
and even that's ironic.
What idiot who's held
a woman's breast
can call it a signifier?
Don't tell me these things
like I've never had a thought.
I'm old
and I want to know
how to love.
The hormonal hallucinations
of my youth
will not suffice.
What is true is that we die.
Soul is the ragged bag
that drags the selves
I've tried to peddle to get by.
Truth may be a fool's
bone rattle but I'm ready
to throw the bones. I'll settle
for a half-truth and let silence
supply the other half.
As for Death, I'll capitalize it.
It becomes truer all the time.
Only longing lasts.

BREAKING THROUGH

At eight, I thought it normal to see music when I listened,
    long bloodlines of strings and fire-burst brass,
        rain-slick street of the cymbals.
Folks thought, *That boy needs help*, and out driving,
        see that red barn, blue sky and gold cone of wood chips,
           is that not a major chord?
You've got to make something something else for it to show up
    in imagination.
Trane, Bird, Cannonball, did it
    and Errol,
forced their instruments past the job description.
    Tatum sweet-talked his hulk of wood and ivory
        like a big tooth horse,
           made it kneel or cantor.
Ornette with his reed menage
      puffed up like a blowfish,
        blew a hive of neon incubi inside your skull.
Diz turned up his flügelhorn to catch the rain in a cistern
    of spangle-gowned mermaids.
Monk wove his brain with Beckett-Kitaj out through his star-fruit fingers.
Left-handed Evans with his modal underwater sculpture
    made *Kind of Blue* his cage of light.
Miles soul-plugged into Dante
    with his extended similes of gold smelt.
Chambers, dream drunk, a heart-lantern in the bar-dark.
Mulligan and Terry trading fours on *Blueport*,
    fine as any Sophoclean stichomythia.
Peggy Lee with her soft hands cupping you where you live,
    whispering
      right up your cock into your heart.
Ella scat-sang altos, flutes, and muted bones and there's Billie
    coming honey-graveled back up the road into the horn's cave,
      like, *Watch this, fools,*
    saxophone got nothin' on me.
Baby, there's a place where love gets tangled up in everything you see.

PRACTICE THIS

After Hafiz

Take any trivial thing and watch it with your heart's eye.
A plastic bunny full of jelly beans, a chocolate egg,
or some creature crawling tremble-legged into the world
from its cocoon. See the way the rain comes up slowly
drop by drop as if checking if the place is safe,
then brings all its friends. Look at your lover after
the glow's worn off and see her as another world
just beginning: this is how it is so often as we rescue
from the mind's long staked out country the fine
strangeness, and kiss it into being: be comforted and fulfilled.

MAGNOLIA

You, there, unnameable, from whose tender center everything
   takes flame.
You open and lift toward me as I approach—tell me your secret
   name.

Magnolia is the appellation of your gown, but who are you that
   opens to me?
I would die today and scatter myself in your shade to know your
   name.

Some are violent with you, bruise your petals and demand you
   speak.
Then another of you opens higher up and out of reach
   protecting your name.

And yet, to me, who am powerless, you surrender your unnamed
   fragrance.
You will stay with me all through my life and I must have your
   holy name.

Metaphors slide from you like rain and science shrinks you to a
   hundred genera.
What do I sing, what wine drink, how dance, to know your secret
   name?

And now your muted grace tells me not to speak, but *be*, and in
   your presence, stay.
There, under my still tongue and everywhere there is silence, is
   your name.

UNTITLED

One day just sat down by the road
and the young man I'd been
kept on running ahead, trumpeting
and spreading his bright feathers,
looking for a new skin to slip on
and I thought, *He's learned nothing*
but what have I got in my little
bone pouch that, when thrown
looks like wisdom, looks like truth?

SIXTY-ONE

Fifty was poignant, heavy pear
departs the tree and the poem
a sigh between branch and mulch.
But no more. Another decade,
I'm all song and scruff,
the mind's hot wire threading joint to joint.
I'll tell you straight out what I think,
no sweetener. Nor has Aphrodite left me
collapsed in a stairwell
and don't you father-flirt me, girl.
This morning the world unbelts her robe,
rose fleshed and randy.
I like the rats that skitter
under the subway's hot rails.
The little black dog
who's afraid of no one,
not even the dope dealer's pit bull.
Montaigne said sickness
is God's way of weaning us from life
but I don't think yet. I like the way
soul clings to gristle like a newspaper
wrapped around a light pole in a storm.
Death's a street away
walking parallel and at my pace. He gets a nod.

ODYSSEUS

It does not happen as they say, the body
sluffing off and leaving light.
No. It's terrible. All those
who came home whole from Troy
now in nursing homes in Argos. Some brat-god
taking back, one by one, each thing they loved.
There is no dignity in this. And so Odysseus
slips from Penelope's warmth in the bed he carved
from a huge tree. Pretending to sleep,
she thinks of the melons she will split
on the courtyard table in the heat of the day.
He steps out into the overcast morning.
She thinks of the joiner's apprentice,
growing to fit his big hands, wonders
if he's had a woman yet.
He feels the cool sand on his feet,
heaves his shoulder into the boat.
She sits up, hangs her feet over the bed.
He is waist high now in the cold water.
Pulls himself up,
yanks the half-hitch, frees the sail.
Rain prickling the swells.
Thunder and surf crash.
I'll not end with my ass wiped by a servant.
She drags something in from outside.
Stares at the bed. Goes at the roots with an ax.

TO THE YOUNG STUDS AT THE GYM

I saw you smirk at the light weights I use,
careful of my scar tissue
and twice-torn tendons. Yes,
behold my ill-chosen workout clothes.
Then you turn away and like cobras
fan your lats at the nubiles
sweating on the bikes.
Go ahead, slide on another plate
and crawl beneath the bar
to best your buddy spotting you.
I hope you make it
a long way into the woods
before life punks you, as it will,
and more than once, and I hope
you'll get up and go another round
each time. But more than that
I'd like to lend you my heart
to carry for a day.
But I wouldn't, no, do that to anyone.

NOT IMPORTANT

Each year I grow emptier,
self sanded away
to a dot in the corner of the frame.
More room here for the night sky.
I can fit a desert in here,
a war, even some old enemies
who've forgotten why
they're angry with me—
Who hurt me? they say,
and besides if not you,
someone else I loved.
There is room for the dead.
They live in my house,
sleep in my bed.
The dogs have stopped barking at them.
The light shines through them
and they brighten.
It's not what you think, they say.

THESEUS

He found the Minotaur dead,
spiderweb grown between the horns.
And then it was for him to sit and think
about the walls of the maze,
the graffiti scrawled there
by those who came before
and left their bones, finally,
at the dead thing's feet.
He was saddened, and asked himself,
What did I miss
in that long passage, lit by such faint light?

PSALM

I left my gift of wine and honey
underneath the olive tree.
Burned the thighs of oxen,
sang and put all of me into it,
but my lover did not come.
She did not come over the plain
with the wind pressing
her gown against her body.
Nor did she arrive and smile
down on my prostrations.
Lord, I heard only the birds
in the branches and felt the wind
cool the sweat on my neck.

I hope I'll die as if I'd swung a pick since dawn
then dipped my cup and disturbed the stars
that swam there in the barrel, so long had been the day,
and full, and my body grateful to lay itself down.

ACKNOWLEDGMENTS

Grateful for the following journals in which many of these poems first appeared:

Azul Editions, Badlands, Cimarron Review, Connecticut Review, Cutthroat, Field, Poetry, Prairie Schooner, Vox Populi, Raleigh Review, San Pedro River Review, The Massachusetts Review, Theodate, Tupelo Quarterly, and *Verdad*.

Much gratitude to Henry Lyman and the Robert Francis Trust for my two-year residency at Fort Juniper, where many of these poems were written.

Thanks to Chard deNiord, Melissa Studdard, Lindsey Royce, the members of Group 18, and Richard Hoffman for their excellent critical responses to the these poems.

 Doug Anderson's book *The Moon Reflected Fire* won the Kate Tufts Discovery Award in 1995, and his *Blues for Unemployed Secret Police* a grant from the Academy of American Poets in 2000. He has received fellowships from the National Endowment for the Arts, the Massachusetts Artists Foundation, Poets & Writers, the *Virginia Quarterly Review*, the MacDowell Colony, and others. He has twice been a fellow at Fort Juniper in Amherst, Massachusetts, the former home of the poet Robert Francis. His play, *Short Timers*, was produced at Theater for the New City in New York in 1981. His memoir, *Keep Your Head Down: Vietnam, the Sixties, and a Journey of Self-Discovery*, was published by W. W. Norton in 2009. He has also written film scripts and criticism. He teaches in the department of comparative literature at the University of Massachusetts–Amherst.

BARROW STREET POETRY

Our Emotions Get Carried Away Beyond Us
Danielle Cadena Deulen (2015)

Radioland
Lesley Wheeler (2015)

Tributary
Kevin McLellan (2015)

Horse Medicine
Doug Anderson (2015)

This Version of Earth
Soraya Shalforoosh (2014)

Unions
Alfred Corn (2014)

O, Heart
Claudia Keelan (2014)

Last Psalm at Sea Level
Meg Day (2014)

Vestigial
Page Hill Starzinger (2013)

You Have to Laugh: New + Selected Poems
Mairéad Byrne (2013)

Wreck Me
Sally Ball (2013)

Blight, Blight, Blight, Ray of Hope
Frank Montesonti (2012)

Self-evident
Scott Hightower (2012)

Emblem
Richard Hoffman (2011)

Mechanical Fireflies
Doug Ramspeck (2011)

Warranty in Zulu
Matthew Gavin Frank (2010)

Heterotopia
Lesley Wheeler (2010)

This Noisy Egg
Nicole Walker (2010)

Black Leapt In
Chris Forhan (2009)

Boy with Flowers
Ely Shipley (2008)

Gold Star Road
Richard Hoffman (2007)

Hidden Sequel
Stan Sanvel Rubin (2006)

Annus Mirabilis
Sally Ball (2005)

A Hat on the Bed
Christine Scanlon (2004)

Hiatus
Evelyn Reilly (2004)

3.14159+
Lois Hirshkowitz (2004)

Selah
Joshua Corey (2003)